smart start

# Alphabet

**Roger Paré**

To Julien

Please visit our web site at: www.garethstevens.com
For a free color catalog describing Gareth Stevens' list of high-quality
books and multimedia programs, call 1-800-542-2595 (USA) or
1-800-461-9120 (Canada). Gareth Stevens Publishing's Fax:
(414) 332-3567.

Library of Congress Cataloging-in-Publication Data available upon
request from publisher. Fax (414) 336-0157 for the attention of the
Publishing Records Department.

ISBN 0-8368-2843-7

This edition first published in 2001 by
**Gareth Stevens Publishing**
A World Almanac Education Group Company
330 West Olive Street, Suite 100
Milwaukee, WI 53212 USA

This edition © 2001 by Gareth Stevens, Inc. Original edition
published in French by Les éditions de la courte échelle inc.,
Montréal, Canada, under the title *L'alphabet* © 1985 Les
éditions de la courte échelle.

Design concept: Derome Design, Inc.
English translation: Patricia Lantier
English text: Dorothy L. Gibbs and Heidi Sjostrom
Cover design: Scott Krall

Printed in the United States of America

1 2 3 4 5 6 7 8 9 05 04 03 02 01

Rykse 1430          3-28-06

**Gareth Stevens Publishing**
A WORLD ALMANAC EDUCATION GROUP COMPANY

# Aa

Two **acrobats** juggle
**apricots** on an **airplane**.

# Bb

A **boa brushes** its **back**
in a **bubblebath**.

# Cc

A **cat** takes a **canary** for a ride in a **canoe**.

# Dd

A **dinosaur dances** with
a **decorated dolphin**.

# Ee

An **enormous elephant**
carries an **emir** to **Egypt**.

# Ff

A **fawn** and its **friends** eat **fruit** in the **forest**.

# Gg

A **gopher** watches a **goofy**
**giraffe** play **golf**.

# Hh

A **handsome hamster** plays
a **harp** and a **harmonica**.

# Ii

An **inquiring insect** carefully **inspects its island**.

# Jj

A **jaguar** drinks some **juice**
in the **jungle**.

# Kk

A **kangaroo** in a **kimono** practices **karate**.

# Ll

A **lion lies** by a **lake** and **licks** its **lips**.

# Mm

A **monster** reads a **martian magazine** on a **motorcycle**.

# Nn

A **nice** girl in **Naples** eats her **noodles neatly**.

# Oo

**Oscar** sings **opera** and sells **oodles** of **oranges**.

# Pp

A **plump pink pig plays**
a **piano** in the **park**.

# Qq

Two **quiet** courtiers **quickly** carry the **queen** to her castle.

# Rr

A **round rat** listens to the **radio** and eats **rice**.

# Ss

A **sculptor snoozes** on the **sand** at a **sunny seashore**.

# Tt

**Tarzan** swings through the **trees** on a **tiger's tail**.

# Uu

This **unusual** horse is wearing a **unique** and **useful uniform**.

# Vv Ww

A **vagabond** plays a **violin**.
**We** listen at the **windows**.

23

# Xx Yy Zz

A **zebra** plays a **xylophone** while eating **yummy yogurt**.

J
P
Par